Daisy Chains

By

Catherine Campbell

ISBN: 9798391606734

Dedicated to:

My boys, Daniel John & Elliot Joe

- you're my inspiration.

[Me]

Would you like to know a little secret?

[Son]

Yes!

[Me]

I'll love you **forever***!*

[Son, a little disappointed]

That's not a secret.

Introduction

When my first son was born, the postnatal report stated it was an *unremarkable* birth. I remember being stunned when I read it - they couldn't have chosen a more inappropriate adjective to describe what just happened.

It struck me, what was so extraordinarily significant and unique in my own life was merely par for the course, in both the medical institutions, and in society at large. After all, every human being that ever walked the earth has a mother, so it's nothing special.

But it is. Anyone who *is* a mother knows that.

In an ideal world, anyone who *has* a mother would know that too. Yet we're told it's *unremarkable*:

> **Unremarkable *[adjective]***
> not worthy of note or attention

Possibly, if it wasn't all so unworthy of attention, we'd see ourselves in a different light. We'd be in awe of ourselves for having executed a miracle in the wake of childbirth.

Under society's watchful eye, it's easy for a new mother to fall into a mindset of comparison, and conformity - or *failure* in the absence of it. A mother learns to measure herself and her child's progress against generalised benchmarks that are essentially meaningless, because very mother, and every child, is unique.

My hope, in sharing my own journey through motherhood in this book, is that it may serve as a reminder to all mothers to stop; allow yourselves time to reflect on what a remarkable journey it's been so far. To allow yourself to indulge in the beauty of it all, as well as walk through the not-so-beautiful with grace and acceptance, knowing you're not alone and you're doing your very best.

I chose daisies to represent this book because they symbolise childbirth, motherhood, and new beginnings. The daisy chain feels like a fitting metaphor to represent the love we have for our children – it has no end.

Catherine Campbell

Table of Contents

0 - 5

And a woman who held a babe against her bosom said,
Speak to us of Children.

And he said:

Your children are not your children.
They are the sons and daughters of Life's longing for itself.
They come through you but not from you,
and though they are with you, yet they belong not to you.
You may give them your love, but not your thoughts,
for they have their own thoughts.
You may house their bodies but not their souls,
for their souls dwell in the house of tomorrow,
which you cannot visit, not even in your dreams.

[Kahlil Gibran – The Prophet]

I'm Different Now

My first son was seven weeks premature, which caught me off guard a little. As a planner and recovering perfectionist, I'd had a clear vision of how it would all play out. I'd give up work a month prior, which would give me time to rest a little as well as finish my 'nesting' and make sure everything was in order for his arrival.

Needless to say, babies don't conform to plan. So, the reality was my waters breaking in the middle of the night, a panic call to the midwife, and an emergency dash to the hospital. My son was born several hours later.

For several weeks, he was in NICU. I wasn't allowed to stay with him at the hospital, so I visited each day to feed and cuddle him, and heartbreakingly, came home each night alone.

This poem is a memory of my first day with him after he *was* home. On reflection, I don't think my new reality fully sank in until then. I'd continued being an 'individual,' leaving the house autonomously for those weeks after he was born, so the impact of suddenly not being able to do that didn't compute until that first day.

I'm Different Now

The first morning I was home alone with my new-born son,
I made myself a cup of tea after putting him down.
There was no milk.
I thought to myself,
What a nuisance, I'll have to go and buy some.

I reached for the car keys.

Then it happened.

I slipped into a different dimension.

I stepped gently out of my body,
turned back towards the bewildered,
wispy outline of myself and whispered,

It's OK.
I understand how you feel.
You can't just go out and get milk whenever you feel like it...
but there's a little something upstairs
you're now willing to die for.
Everything has changed.

And as I watched the wisp of me evaporate,
my heart was grateful for her -
- grateful she had delivered me to this place.

Heartbeat Symphony

When a little heartbeat starts
inside your body,
a symphony is born.

It goes a little like this…

ppp	as pianissimo as possible
pp	pianissimo (very soft)
p	piano (soft)
mp	mezzo piano (moderately soft)
mf	mezzo forte (moderately loud)
f	forte (loud)
ff	fortissimo (very loud)
fff	as fortissimo as possible

When it reaches its crescendo,
and the little heartbeat
leaves your body,
the symphony remains in your heart,
and plays when you least expect it...
sometimes pianissimo
and sometimes **FORTISSIMO**

A Mothers Love

When you become a mother,
the word *love* takes on a new dimension.

It isn't the kind of love you feel for your parents.

It isn't the kind of love you feel for your best friend.

It isn't the kind love you feel for your lover.

It isn't the kind of love you feel for whatever else it is that you love, like perhaps chocolate, or salt and vinegar crisps.

It's nothing like that.

It's something deep and visceral,
because it's born *inside* you.
It doesn't come from an external source.

It's kept alive by your very own breath.

It's nourished by your very own energy.

It's two hearts in one body.

It is a love that touches you in places you've never been touched –
on the inside.

This is the dimension of love only a mother can know.

Changes

The sentiment in this poem is very real. When I fell pregnant with my first son, I was a Project Manager responsible for the global implementation of a new software system. The budget was several million dollars, and the deadlines were strict. My level of accountability was high, but I always felt energised by the challenge rather than stressed.

Enter baby boy. Suddenly, the most basic task of counting how many bottles of milk I had to make caused me unparalleled anxiety and stress. I felt like my orderly, sharp, energised brain had been consumed by a giant fluffy cloud, where any attempt to grasp facts or reason left me flailing around blind.

I'd never anticipated feeling such an absolute shift. Having a child gave me a perspective that made the accountability I had for my work project pale into insignificance, compared with the accountability I now had for a little human being, of my own making.

Changes

I've been to university -
a management degree...
but you, my wondrous little boy,
have totally befuddled me.

I've worked on global projects -
advanced progressively...
but you, my cheeky little boy,
have totally unravelled me.

I've travelled all around the world -
by plane and train, and sea...
but you, my carefree little boy,
have totally bedazzled me.

My composition's changing...
it's all so very new -
and that's because, my darling boy,
I'm simply so in love with you.

Brothers in Arms

My second son was born when my first was three. There was heightened anticipation over his arrival as I'd been admitted to hospital for a complication several weeks prior to his due date. It meant I didn't get to see much of my three-year old during that time as he could only come in visiting hours. We'd talk about his brother-to-come and he would tell me about what kind of brother he wanted to be. He was genuinely excited and never showed any sign of feeling worried, jealous, or displaced.

This poem is written about my memory of the day he came to visit his little brother in hospital for the first time.

Brothers in Arms

When you held your brother in your arms -
you were three,
and he'd been in the world for twelve hours.

You were an incredibly thoughtful little boy -
so often in your own world,
contemplating deep mysteries.

I knew you had been quietly contemplating his arrival -

never with any hint of jealousy or fear,
only with deep anticipation
and awe of a pending miracle.

You were soon to become a big brother -
and that was *indeed,*
a big responsibility.

You sat on the chair by my hospital bed,
and let me whisper to you secrets of how to hold him.
I lowered him into your arms.

Your face,
I will never forget.
I saw every single emotion you felt -

astonishment

pride

uncertainty

vulnerability

responsibility
awe

love

In that moment,
I witnessed a pure and beautiful connection of souls.

My own intense emotions,
having just given birth to your brother,
were overwhelmed in that moment with pride,
and love for you.

I knew in that moment,
without a doubt,
what an amazing big brother you would be.

Ask Your Father

Both of my children are "why" boys. I say 'are' rather that *were* because they still are. When my first son started with the questions, my own Mum thought it was hilarious karma, as apparently, I used to drive her insane with my own incessant questioning.

Early on, the questions were generally quite basic and easy to answer. I was all over it. Then some tricky questions started to creep in, which I had to defer answering on the spot so I could do a quick google enquiry before I got back to them, such as "*How do snails work?*"

Because the questions were never ending, eventually I ran out of time to keep up the charade I knew all the answers. I knew at some point the boys would realise I didn't *actually* know everything. Sadly, it came sooner than expected due to their inquisitive nature.

I remember the first time I responded with,

"I don't know."

I thought that admission would make me feel as though I was letting them down, or that somehow the light would go out in their eyes when they looked at me, because I was merely a shadow of the omniscient being I pretended to be. But in truth, it was very liberating. I learned the value of being honest with them, which is what I'd always insisted they were with me.

Ask Your Father

"Mama, how do planets grow?"
Ask you father, he will know.

"Mama, why's the earth not flat?"
Ask your father, he'll know that.

"Mama, does a slug have eyes?"
Ask your father, he'll advise.

"Mama, what keeps up a plane?"
Ask your father, he'll explain.

"Mama, who invented glue?"
Ask your father, he'll know who.

"Mama, how do babies grow?"
That, my darling, that I know!

Hint of You

You're just a cheeky hint of you,
my darling, funny son...
a hint of something wonderful –
– your journey just begun.

You're just a sneaky wink of you,
my darling, sparkly son...
a hint of something fabulous –
your future still to come.

You're just a fleeting glimpse of you,
my darling, lively son,
a hint of something beautiful –
the man that you'll become.

What You See

I see a hill.

You see a mountain, imagining what a fabulous adventure it would be to scale its height and stick a rainbow flag at the peak.

It makes you want to be an adventurer when you grow up.

I see a lizard.

You see a dinosaur's grandchild, descended from an unimaginable world of prehistoric wonder and magnificence.

It makes you want to be an archaeologist when you grow up.

I see a plane.

You see people moving through the clouds, suspended miraculously between the earth and who-knows-how-far-up-it-goes.

It makes you want to be an astronaut when you grow up.

I see a building.

You see a structure towering in splendour,
with beautiful bones and glistening glass,
and wonder how it's even possible to build such a thing.

It makes you want to be an engineer when you grow up.

I see stars.
You see a universe.

Darling, whatever you become when you grow up,
never forget - there are infinite possibilities
beyond what the eye can see.

5 - 10

Do not confine your children
to your own learning.
For they have been born
In another time.

[Hebrew Proverb]

First Impressions

I found this in my little *things-I-can't-throw-away* box, and it reminded me how uncomplicated things used to be.

It's the top three things my five-year-old loved about me. If he doesn't remember numbers 1 and 3, I do hope he'll always remember number 2!

First Expenditure

This poem is a memory I have of my son getting his first wallet for his birthday. It had a velcro strip and was Kermit the frog green, with a crisp five dollar note inside. One of his birthday activities was going to the circus with some friends. I told him if he saw anything he'd like to buy with his five dollars, he should treat himself for his birthday. There were clowns walking up and down the tiered seating area, with baskets of handheld fans around their necks, which lit up in rainbow colours when you started the fan. My son was memorised by them. I'll never forget the look on his face when he looked up at me with starry anticipation in his eyes, and said,

"*Mum, do you think I can buy one of those with my money*?"

Serendipitously, the price was five dollars. He'd never bought anything by himself before, so the idea of using his wallet and making the purchase independently was incredibly exciting for him. I could also see in his eyes he was anxious about having to make the approach without me, but I encouraged him to do it.

We also had our first little conversation that day about money and 'value.' I asked him whether he'd rather go home with his five dollars still to spend on something else, or if the fan was worth that much to him. He thought about it, and decided the fan was worth it.

For some reason, what happened that day, particularly watching him approach the clown and make the transaction on his own, remains a vivid memory. I felt every inch of his excitement, anxiety, and ultimate pride, which I saw in his confident stride as he walked back to me with his fan, wallet empty.

First Expenditure

I remember your birthday,
the burst of your pride -
a little green wallet, five dollars inside.

I remember the circus,
the fizz in the air -
a little green wallet, five dollars to spare.

I remember the juggler,
the beam on your face -
a little green wallet, five dollars encased.

I remember the fanlights,
you asked my advice -
a little green wallet, five dollars their price!

I remember dilemma,
the choice you then made -
a little green wallet, five dollars you paid.

I remember your bedtime,
your utter delight -
a little green wallet,
no dollars, but light!

The Other Mothers

My son turned five not long after we moved to a new region of the country. Consequently, starting school was a leap of faith beyond what's expected, as he wasn't going with any of the friends he'd already made prior to us moving. Likewise, the neighbourhood was new to me, so I didn't know any families in the area.

My son was relaxed about starting school – it was me who felt a little anxious about the whole thing. I felt socially awkward back then, uncomfortable amongst people I didn't know. I felt out of place dropping him at school and waiting outside the classroom for him at the end of the day. I'd stand on the fringe, often with headphones on, or pretending to be interested in a tree or something, all the time conscious the 'other mothers' were laughing and having fun together, like they'd known each other their whole lives.

On reflection, I'm sure there will have been mothers like me, feeling the same. Now I realise my view of the in-crowd was distorted by my own anxiety, but it took me a long time to understand that. At the time, I felt the 'other mothers' were supremely confident and had the motherhood gig perfectly under control. Having become friends with some of them over the years that followed, I can say it was all an illusion. You can never have everything perfectly under control when you're a mother. It doesn't work like that.

This is a poem about the observations and thoughts I had in those early school days.

The Other Mothers

The *Other Mums* cut circles,
their apples don't have pips...
it's never just a carrot,
it's carrot sticks, with dips.

The *Other Mums* wear lipstick,
have time to brush their hair...
they stop and talk to teachers,
compare their active wear.

The *Other Mums* host parties,
designing every treat...
bake birthday cakes of legends,
make party bags elite.

The *Other Mums* do coffees,
and evening meets with wine...
discuss ideas to fund raise,
and offer up their time.

I'm the *Other Mother,*
my sandwiches are square.
Sometimes, when I drive to school,
I'm still in underwear.

I'm not a fan of baking -
I always make mistakes.
I don't like planning parties,
and buy the birthday cakes.

But hey, we're all just mothers,
giving all we've got...
and some things, we are good at,
and other things, we're not.

Long Car Trips

I don't think this one needs an introduction – for any parent who has ever endured a long car trip with children, it speaks for itself!

I spy, with my little eye,
something beginning with T...
and NO, it's not tiredness, or tyres, or time,
it has to be something you *SEE.*

I spy, with my little eye,
something beginning with B...
and NO, it's not breathing, or boredom, or brains,
it has to be something you *SEE.*

I spy, with my little eye,
something beginning with P...
and NO, it's not puffiness, patience, or pulse,
it has to be something you *SEE.*

I spy, with my little eye,
something beginning with D...
and NO, it's not diligence, dust mites, or draft,
it has to be something you *SEE.*

I spy, with my little eye...
oh, never mind.

Winner

Neither of my boys were sporty. They would much rather have played boardgames on a Saturday morning than be on a sports field. It didn't stop them trying though. My younger son loved playing hockey – how I remember those frosty weekend mornings, where the youngest teams got the earliest time slots.

I was the same when I was young - always the last to get picked for a team. Having to participate in the annual athletic and cross-country sports days used to make me feel physically sick. It helped me to understand my boys, and while I encouraged them to try different things, I never put any pressure on them. When a sports day came up at their school, I knew what they felt, and did my best to explain it was about participation and while they might not be very good at running, there *were* good at so many other things, and you can't be good at everything.

I was always very proud of them for giving it their best shot. They never tried to dodge out of it, they just got on with it.

This is a poem describing how I used to feel waiting on the school field for them to finish the cross-country.

Winner

Where is he?
I'm feeling a little anxious now -
all the other boys are across the line.

No-one is even watching the race anymore,
as though it's over.

"*It's not over*!" I want to yell,
because *you're* not across the line yet.

When I see you turn the corner,
my heart pushes against my chest,
urgent to break free - to reach you,
and draw you home.

The 'snail crusher' teacher cruises behind you.
Is it impatience, or humour,
I see on her face?
Either way, I'm the only one still watching.
Either way, I'm quietly grateful she's had your back.

As you come closer, I see your beetroot face,
beads of sweat on your brow.
Your unwieldy legs, not fit for purpose,
trying their best beneath your parachute shorts.

You meet my eyes, and beam.

I see you, my love.
I see you.

In that moment, the love I feel for you almost breaks me.

I high-five you at the finish line, and hand you an ice block with such nonchalance, you'd never imagine I'd run every step of that race with you.

When you've caught your breath, you chuckle and say,

"*Well Mum, at least I beat the snail crusher*!"

That's when I know you're OK.

That's when I know you'll always be a winner – because you lost with such grace and good humour.

As your face regains its natural colour,
so too my heart resumes its natural position.

15 Reasons

I've always told my boys not to buy me anything for Mother's Day, but rather make me something, or do something kind for me.

This is a list my son gave me on Mother's Day when he was 7 years old. When I discovered it recently, I felt overwhelmed remembering the love we shared back then. I'd forgotten what kind of Mum I was, and what our relationship was like. As the boys have grown, they've been many times I've thought about actions I took, or decisions I made when they were younger, and felt regret. I've ruminated over specific incidents, where on reflection I realise I could/*should* have done things differently – in a more effective, rational, or kinder way.

Rediscovering this list helped me gain a new perspective. Perfection is impossible, in life and in motherhood. When we put a spotlight on the 'bad' incidents, all the good stuff falls into the dark, forgotten. In reality, the vast majority of what we've done is nothing short of spectacular, and that's what we need to remember.

If my son genuinely felt these things in his heart when he was 7 years old, then he's OK. And that means *I* did OK.

The list is written *exactly* as he wrote it:

15 reasons why I love my mum

1. she's all ways kind
2. when I ask her to do something she Hardley ever says "no"
3. she looks Beatiful
4. when I tell her something she always understands
5. she always turks me in Bed on night time
6. she has a good sense of humor
7. she gives me lots of kisses
8. and lots of hugs
9. today is mothers day
10. she hardley ever get mad or angrey
11. I think shes the 1st = Best person in the world
12. we allways will love each other
13. she aprecheates my fellings
14. the fact that I just love her
15. this list (see numbers 1-15)

Absent Minded Boy

I wrote my son a bedtime story when he was very young, called *Daniel John with One Sock On*. It was an in-joke for us as he was forever sock-less (always his left foot), and the missing socks could never be found. It was like the 8th wonder of the modern world. That trait was the start of a pattern in his behaviour. More than the average boy, he would mysteriously lose things.

This poem is a nod to that quality, which I wrote many years later after connecting the dots. He was always in his own little world - a thinker and a dreamer. And one who dreams has far more important things to think about than where they left their left sock.

Absent Minded Boy

Daniel John.
One sock on.
One sock gone.

I was constantly bewildered about
where your other sock might be.

You never noticed, of course -
your thoughts were consumed with far more important matters.

I understood very early in our relationship
how unique you were -
my very own little absent-minded professor.

I can't tell you how many lunchboxes you lost at school.
To this day, I can't comprehend how it's even possible
to lose so many lunchboxes.

Getting dressed, you always wore the first thing you laid eyes on, which made it very easy for me to manipulate your choices, whilst pretending I enabled your initiative.
Contemplation over style, or social acceptance
has never been your thing.

After all, there were far more important matters to be contemplating.

The length of time you took to put your shoes on
when we left the house was unfathomable.
One shoe on.
One shoe gone.

Whenever we went out, without fail,
your hat, or wallet,
or some other equally critical item
would be declared absent at the destination,
despite an abundance of suggestions prior to departure
you might like to bring it along.

This is the way of absent-minded professors.

You have a gift, Daniel John.

You've always instinctively known that where your lunchbox
is or what clothes you wear are very *unimportant* things.

Your mind isn't designed for such minutiae.
It's designed to wonder where ants go
when they disappear down pavement cracks -
why some people still believe the earth is flat -
why negative thoughts seem easier
to hold on to than positive ones -
and other such critical matters.

And knowing you, Daniel John,
with your one sock on,
and one sock gone,
you'll figure it all out.

Very Important Thoughts

"Mama,"

Yes, darling?

"I'm having an important thought."

Oh wow, would you like to share it with me?

"I'm not sure."

OK love, you think about it. I'm here if you decide you'd like to.

"OK."

[30 seconds later]

"Mama,"

Yes, darling?

"I think I'd like to share my important thought."

OK love, just when you're ready.

[child pause]

"I don't think Father Christmas is real."

Gosh darling, I agree, that really is *a very important thought!*

"I think it's you."

[mother pause]

What makes you think that love?

"It's just a feeling."

[much longer mother pause – trying to decide in that
moment what's the most appropriate thing to say next.
Will he be upset I've lied to him all this time?
Will the joy be sucked out of Christmas now?
Will he tell his friends?
This is BIG!]

***We can talk about this a bit more when we get home
if you like love, but you're right, it is me.
You were right to trust your feelings and share that very
important thought with me.***

"Can we get an ice-cream on the way home?"

True Magic

This poem is connected to "Very Important Thoughts" in terms of whether we do right by our children in pretending Father Christmas is real, or the Easter Bunny, or the Tooth Fairy. I was always worried when my children found out none of it was *real*, I'd be exposed for lying, which is the very thing I'd told them not to do under any circumstances. It's always been something that's made me feel a little uneasy because it feels hypocritical.

With Christmas in particular though, it's hard *not* to participate in the fantasy when the rest of society is doing it - with Father Christmas's dressed up in shopping malls, and reindeer food for sale. Despite my own uncertainty around whether it was 'technically' the right thing to indulge in, I played along for my boys because I could appreciate how much joy and excitement it brought them. I also didn't want them to be the ones at school proclaiming Father Christmas wasn't real and spoiling it for everyone else.

True Magic

As a little girl, I remember believing in Christmas,
until a boy on my school bus told me it was all lies,
and I was silly for believing.

I remember my son believing in Christmas too,
until that day in the car, when he said he had
something important to tell me.

Would my response in that moment
crush his unwavering belief in magic?

I've been exposed as a liar.

My children wholeheartedly believed that once a year a man
living in the North Pole embarked on a magical journey,
surfing waves of stardust to deliver presents to every other
living child.

They believed, without a shadow of doubt, that magic
happened.

Are we, as parents, propagators of deceit,
or magic weavers?

We held their little hands and took them on an otherworldly,
spellbinding journey, where they became the main character
in a real-life fairy tale.

We put sparkles in their eyes and tinsel in their souls.

We gifted them the kind of trembling anticipation and
excitement that leads to loss of sleep -

their eyes not wanting to miss what comes next as their little
hearts swell to bursting on the eve of a miracle.

Who doesn't want their child to feel that?

The feeling is very real - even if the story isn't.

That's why *I* remember believing in Christmas.
Because I remember the *feeling*.

As a parent, I used to wonder whether it was right
to 'lie' about magic.
I've concluded though, my failing might have been
in not telling the *truth* about magic...
in failing to explain it's all around us.

I should have taught my children that magic is what happens
every time a flower grows from a seed –
that magic is what happens
every time a baby is born –
that magic is what happens
every time you breathe in just the right composition of air
to fill your lungs and keep you alive -
that *true* magic is as real as Father Christmas is not.

Imagine what life would be like if our children grew up
allowing themselves to be filled with the same sense of
anticipation and euphoria about everyday things...

That they might wake to see a rose unfurled in the garden, and feel the same joy as they would waking to see a present waiting for them under an artificial tree.

Imagine that.

From Son to Mum

This is a poem my son surprised me with when I came home from hospital after having back surgery. He was 9 years old. I'd written little notes and poems for him since he was old enough to read, so was incredibly proud to realise he'd put his own mind to this! He still writes poetry now.

The poem is written exactly as he wrote it:

THIS IS QUITE AN INTERESTING SUM:
KINDNESS + HAPPINESS = MUM.
SHE IS A HALF TRAINED STUDENT TUTOR
AND SOMETIMES LETS ME ON THE COMPUTER.

I LOVE HER ALLOT, SHE LOVES ME BACK
SHE'S SOMETIMES STRICT AND SOMETIMES SLACK.
SHE CURRENTLY HAS A VERY SORE BACK
SHE SHOULD JUST RELAX AND HAVE A SNACK.

SHE HAS AN AWESOME SON NAMED DANIEL
SHE HAS TWO PUPPIES WHO ARE NOT SPANIELS.
SOMETIME I WISH THAT THEY WOULD GO MUTE
BUT THEY STILL ARE KINDA CUTE.

SHE MAKES ALL MOMENTS TURN ALL FUN,
I LOVE HER TO BITS CAUSE SHE'S MY MUM.

FROM YOUR FAVOURITE SON.

10 - 16

And a woman who held a babe against her bosom said,
Speak to us of Children.

And he said:

You may strive to be like them,
but seek not to make them like you.
For life goes not backward nor tarries with yesterday.
You are the bows from which your children,
as living arrows are sent forth.
The archer sees the mark upon the path of the infinite,
and He bends you with His might that His arrows
may go swift and far.
Let your bending in the archer's hand be for gladness;
For even as He loves the arrow that flies,
so He loves also the bow that is stable.

[Kahlil Gibran – The Prophet]

Russian Dolls

Today I came across a photo of you in the kitchen drawer.

It was a photo I'd come across many times before, each time mindlessly sweeping it aside as I searched for the thing I was looking for.

Today though, you caught my eye, and I pulled you out and looked back at you.

My body went into a kind of quiet shock,
and time stopped,
and I forgot what I had come for.

I was flooded with an overwhelming sense of grief.
My tears came from a deep and sacred place – somewhere I'd forgotten existed but was very much alive.

I couldn't breathe.

Where are you now?

What happened to you?

My heart ached, and I wished I could have just one more day with you, as you were.
I'd promise to remember everything.

When it stopped, I put you back into the drawer.

I took a deep breath and reminded myself you're still that little boy – only a bigger version.

The thing about being your Mum is that I'm the keeper of all versions of you, starting from the very beginning.

Like Russian dolls.

You started inside me, and year upon year,
layer upon layer,
you grew into newer, bigger versions of yourself.
And as each layer emerged, the last was encased,
never to be seen again.

All those versions of you stand as individuals in my heart.
I'm blessed to have known them all intimately;
to have loved them all.

Some days, like today,
I'm reminded of one of them.
And I remember how much I loved him,
I miss him.

Mum

Here's another poem my son wrote to me – this time for my birthday when he was 11 years old. I treasure it now because he was on the cusp of adolescence, so it represents the final trace of uninhibited expression from boy to Mum.

The poem is written exactly as he wrote it:

Whether I'm sad, angry, or even struck with fear,

it's nice to know that I have a mother who is always there.

She is full of idioms & a lot of quotes,

She remembers many things, as she makes a note.

She has travelled near and far, (sometimes even with me).

and not long after we get home I make her a cup of tea.

She have two lovely dogs, one molly and one ebony.

She's trustworthy and honest, always true to her identity.

She makes other people happy, even when there sad.

Happiness is something that she never fail to add.

The jokes she tells will easily make me laugh and smile.

I love the way she tells them, and her humorous stile

She is conscious of my safety, always quite aware,

as oppose to all those mothers who simply just don't care.

I know your back is not the best and hope that it gets better,

And hope that you enjoyed reading this letter.

Sidekicks in Time

You really loved me.
so mutch!
You wrote in the little love letters we traded.

Our time together was so memorable,
and meaningful,
and beautiful.

We spent hours in the bath,
making magical, colourful potions,
then cast spells on each other.
The green spells always came true for you.

We grew strawberries and beanstalks,
hunted for worms and tracked reindeer,
and slid carefree down the spine of terrifying dragons.

We flew in rocket ships,
rode bareback on hippopotamuses and unicorns,
and explored underground caves.

We built castles,
then teared them down with our bare hands.

We were trusty sidekicks,
laughing, and living fearlessly in the moment.

I had your back.
And you had mine.

[Twelve years later]

I'm the very last person in the world you'd want to have an adventure with.

In fact, if I *was* the very last person in the world,
you'd choose to venture without me.

Some days, I'm struck by the memory
of *us*...

And I really miss you...
so mutch.

I Miss Your Shoes

I knew this would happen -
that I'd miss your shoes by the front door,
though I'd cursed them a thousand times for tripping me up.
I *knew* it.

I knew this would happen -
that I'd miss seeing light stream into the hallway
from under your bedroom door,
though it made me irritable you were still up when you had
school the next day.
I *knew* it.

I knew this would happen -
that I'd miss playing monopoly with you,
though I'd rather have stuck pins in my eyes
than play monopoly ever again in this life.
I *knew* it.

I knew this would happen -
that I'd miss hearing your incessant chatter,
though it drove me to despair when I was trying to watch T.V.
I *knew* it.

I knew this would happen -
that I'd miss seeing your bike in the garage.
though I'd clench my fists every time I had to move it
to get washing in the machine.

I *knew* it.

I knew this would happen -
that I'd miss hearing you come home late in the weekends,
though I'd wake startled,
skin pricked with fear hearing doors bang.

I *knew* it.

I *knew* this would happen.

I miss your voice.
I miss your face.
I miss you here, with me...
even more than I knew I would.

Driving to Work

I saw you today.

You were holding hands with me walking to preschool, chattering away while making sure you didn't step on a pavement crack in case your dreams didn't come true.

Well, it wasn't really you, but it used to be.

It made me remember how incredibly proud I was of you and the young boy you were becoming.

I saw you today.

You were walking to school, head bobbing just above your gigantic backpack, water bottle swinging off the side. You stopped every so often to contemplate where the ants go, or some other great mystery.

Well, it wasn't really you, but it used to be.

It made me remember how fearful I was the first day you walked to school alone - ducking behind bushes so you didn't see I was following you...
acting so very nonchalant as you walked through the front door after school, like I hadn't been staring out the window for a sighting of your gigantic backpack in the driveway.

I saw you today.

You were sitting on the back seat of the bus,

your nonstop jiggling and kiwifruit haircut giving you away.

Well, it wasn't really you, but it used to be.

It made me remember how anxious I felt when you caught the school bus the first time -
worried a big kid might jostle you, or swear,
or talk about something too startling for your young ears.

I saw you today.

You were riding your bike slowly along the footpath,
legs like a new-born foal sticking out of shorts that looked as though you might take flight any minute -
plenty of room for growth.

Well, it wasn't really you, but it used to be.

It made me remember how terrified I felt the first day you rode your bike to school -
worried you'd lose your way or fall off and no one would be there to help you.

I saw you today.

You were riding your bike at speed,
hands-free along the road.
Inappropriate socks, worn intentionally in protest of uniform rules and unkept hair tumbling down your back.
No helmet.

Well, it wasn't really you, but it used to be.

It made me remember how unsettled I felt,
wondering if you might be inclined to break more serious rules or take bigger risks I wouldn't be privy to.

I saw you today.

You were walking to university in confident stride,
slim backpack hanging loosely off your broad shoulders,
cup of Starbucks in hand.

Well, it wasn't really you, but it could have been.

It made me realise how incredibly proud I am of you still,
and of the young man you are becoming.

All these memories,
all these feelings...
delivered to me within moments,
as I drove to work today.

Holding On

I feel like I’m losing my son.
It’s as though he’s constantly driven to fight against me.

I don’t know what to do.

I don’t know what to do.

I feel like I’m trying to reel in a big fish.
He wrestles to break away so he can swim freely.

It's pure instinct.
I know that.

I’m starting to think I need to let him go.

Even if I execute every move to precision,
it's likely he'll break.
We’re both exhausted.

I’m starting to think I need to let him go.

I tell myself he'll swim back freely when he's ready.

I tell myself he'll know exactly where to find me –
still at the other end of that line,
where I’ve always been.

Only when he finds me again, I'll be a little different.

I'll be cloaked with the courage and vulnerability
it took, to let him go.

I See You

This poem is very close to my heart. I wrote it for my son when he was 16. He expressed a need to spend time away from me, which was heart-breaking at the time. On reflection he did the right thing for us both, and I'm grateful for that now. When it happened, I was torn between being incredibly frustrated with him and insanely proud he had the strength of character to do what he believed was right for himself, without compromise. That's a lesson it can take some people a lifetime to learn, if at all.

At the time, I genuinely believed I was helping him, giving him advice about how to work through some difficulties he was having. I failed miserably and got it wrong at every turn. I tried to be empathetic by putting myself in his shoes - I believed I *had* been in his shoes, and therefore knew what was best for him. That was my mistake.

What I know now having come out the other end of it, is I should never have presumed I could be in his shoes, or know what he felt like, or what he was going through. Because I'm not him. For me, it was a crisis that led to a pivotal moment in our relationship, as well as my identity as a mother. I felt there was so much I needed to share with him, but they were *my* needs, not his. What *he* needed was to figure out who he was *without me.*

It was excruciatingly difficult to let him go. After sixteen years of guiding him and helping him navigate his way through challenges, it stopped, just like that. It left me flailing as a mother. As he'd set himself free to find himself, the equal and opposite reaction was that I lost myself.

It was during this time I began writing again, after not having written for many years. Poetry has always been my sanctuary – the place I go when I need comfort and support. It enables me to share feelings I couldn't otherwise verbalise or express. It helps me to process mixed or intense thoughts, enabling them to find a resting place. I'll forever be grateful his decision to take space liberated us both.

I See You

I see you, darling.

I know you feel misunderstood.

I want so much to tell you I *do* understand.
Not all of it, but the part about what it feels like trying to carve your way through a world that isn't designed for you.

You think so much.

You care so deeply.

You *feel* everything.

And it feels like you're the only one feeling everything,
and it feels like you're the only one caring so deeply.
The weight is so heavy you can't even put words to it,
so you carry it inside while trying to meet
all the expectations of this misfit world.

You are a teenager, grandson, friend, brother, and son.

You are not yet yourself.

It's painfully difficult to find yourself
when you've needed to wear so many disguises,
and act on so many stages.

I think that's what makes you feel angry sometimes -
you know the real You is close,
because you hear him whisper off stage.
But whenever you've reached for him,
he's slipped through your fingers.

Having to be all those other 'You-s" is draining,
and you've not had the strength to pull him into you.
Until now.

Now you have a grip on him,
and can look him in the eye for the first time.

He has beautiful eyes.

He has passion in his heart and fire in his soul.

He is the kind of person who is courageous enough to put himself first by putting aside expectations others have of him, because he has important work to do getting to know himself.

As someone who also feels and cares deeply,
I understand how intense and consuming
this work of getting to know yourself is.

I understand you must make sacrifices to give it your full attention - the kind that means perhaps you can't be a grandson, a brother or son for a while.

And that's OK.

I'll be right where you left me,
excited to meet the new You.

I will love you with all my heart,
no more or less than all the other little versions of You
I've already loved,
and all future versions of You
yet to reveal themselves.

I see you, darling.

17 - 20

All the art of living
lies in a fine mingling, of letting go
and holding on.

[Henry Havelock Ellis]

Vital Signs

After my first child was born, I found myself asking Mum
about my own 'very important' milestones as a toddler:

How old was I when I said my first word and what was it?

What was my favourite bedtime story?

Did I enjoy finger foods, and what was my favourite?

When did I take my first step and who was there?

What was my favourite toy?

Her answer was always the same and every time,
it took me by surprise,

"Oh gosh, I have no idea love; it was a long time ago."

It made me think she can't have paid much attention, or those
milestones clearly weren't *memorable* enough to remember.
It made me sad she had forgotten such important things.

My baby was my universe - and all these questions,
and all these milestones were in its atmosphere.

These were *vital signs*,
and critical achievements.
Yet my own Mum couldn't remember mine.

What kind of mother did that make her?

I for one, would certainly never forget these things about my *own* child.
Never.

What kind of mother would that make me?

[Twenty years later]

Now I'm the *kind of Mother* who can't tell you how old my son was when he said his first word, or what it was.

I'm the *kind of Mother* who can't tell you what his favourite finger food was, or when he took his first step,
and who was there.

What kind of Mother does that make me?

It makes me the kind of mother who knows she invested every cell of her own essence,
and infinite love into her child when he was a baby.

It makes me the kind of mother who was able to be fully present and embrace the joy of first words, first steps, and favourite bedtime stories, without feeling the need to lock it in the memory bank for recall in 20 years-time.

It makes me the kind of mother who now understands she shouldn't have judged her own mother for things she didn't understand when she was a new mother herself.

It's OK that I don't remember the finer details of that time.

It's OK.

I remember the *feeling*, and that's enough.

I Get It Now

The day my son came inside out,
it altered me, without a doubt -
- and rather unexpectedly,
my heart crashed through the wall of me.

His day of birth, I changed somehow.
I get it, Mum.
I get it now.

The day he broke his fragile bone,
I felt it crack, as if my own -
and rather understandably,
I wished his pain belonged to me.

It wasn't fair on him, somehow.
I get it, Mum.
I get it now.

The day he walked to school alone,
like MI5, I tracked him home -
I acted calm, but secretly,
relief swept through the veins of me.

I took that leap of faith, somehow.
I get it, Mum.
I get it now.

The day he learned to drive a car,
I hoped he wouldn't venture far -
and rather uncontrollably,
a cloak of fear fell over me.

He felt too young to drive, somehow.
I get it, Mum.
I get it now.

The day his lover broke his heart,
I felt my own had ripped apart.
Instinctively, protectively,
I longed to wrap him up in me.

I had to ease his pain, somehow.
I get it, Mum.
I get it now.

The day he flew from feathered nest,
my heart launched with him, from my chest.
I felt alone, but equally,
a swell of pride washed over me.

I'd helped him learn to fly, somehow.
I get it, Mum.
I get it now.

Mum, you told me, as I grew,
I'd need my own, before I knew…
you'd squeeze me gently by the hand,
and say, "One day, you'll understand."

I get it, Mum,
I really do.

And Mum, at last,
I get you too.

Through the Years

At *one,*
I carried you.
I took you everywhere I went.
You were my unconditional little cuddle buddy -
the absolute centre of my world.
I loved you fiercely.

At *five,*
I held your hand.
I let you go in good faith, enabling you to wander cautiously,
yet freely into your first magnificent solo adventures.
I loved you fiercely.

At *ten,*
I encouraged you.
I helped you find your own little light,
and showed you how to keep it shining -
when others tried to blow it out.
I loved you fiercely.

At *fifteen,*
I watched you.
I became a shadow, observing you from a distance,
like a hawk ready to swoop
the second I thought you were in trouble -

trying so very hard to glide about nonchalantly,
and not swoop in by accident.
I loved you fiercely.

At *eighteen*,
I empowered you.
I assisted you on your way,
then watched with tremendous pride,
as you left confidently to begin the rest of your life.
I loved you fiercely.

At *twenty*,
You don't need me to carry you anymore -
- you carry yourself just beautifully.

You don't need me to hold your hand anymore -
though I hope you'll always have someone in your life
who will.

You don't need me to encourage you anymore -
your light is blazing, and everyone can see it.

You don't need me to watch over you anymore -
I trust you'll find me if you're ever in trouble.

You don't need me to empower you anymore -
because you know in your heart how capable you are.

You don't *need* me to do any of these things for you now - but know this... I would.

In a heartbeat.

Because I love you fiercely.

Days of Motherhood

I didn't hold your hand that day.
Because
while I was on a mission, you were dawdling...
paying extraordinary attention to the ants crawling into pavement cracks,
without consideration for my schedule.

So frustrating.
I'm sorry darling.
I dawdle sometimes too now, and it would be nice for someone to hold my hand, without trying to rush me.

I asked you to stop talking that day.
Because
while I was craving silence, you were babbling...
incessantly speaking your every thought out loud to anyone who would listen,
without consideration for my sanity.

So aggravating.
I'm sorry darling.
I speak my thoughts out loud sometimes too now,
and love it when people listen, without interruption.

I told you I wouldn't play a game with you that day.
Because
while I was busy, you were bored...
interrupting me constantly,
only interested in entertaining yourself,
without consideration for my agenda.

So irritating.
I'm sorry darling.
I get bored sometimes too now and would love nothing more than to play a game with you, without time restriction.

I asked you to go away and leave me alone that day.
Because
while I needed space, you needed company...
following me around, jumping all over me, smothering me,
without consideration for my personal space.

So agitating.
I'm sorry darling.
I have all the space I need now, and would love nothing more than your company, without conditions.

When you're a mother,
some days *are* -
frustrating, aggravating, and irritating.

Those days were difficult.

However,
there were vastly more days,
my love,
when we *did* hold hands,
and share thoughts,
and play games,
and cuddle.

Those days were the best days of my life.

To Whom It May Concern

A father gives away the bride; his daughter - duty done.
I wonder when a mother, then,
should give away her son?

I'd like to give my son away with more than just a kiss.
And so, *To Whom He Gives Himself,*
to You, I give you this:

I give to you his ocean eyes, which first gazed into mine.
I give to you his mark of birth,
uniquely our design.

I give to you his graceful hands,
which tucked in mine for years.
I give to you his battle scars,
each carved from childhood tears.

I give to you his gifted mind,
which learned to read with ease.
I give to you his outstretched arms,
which brought me to my knees.

I give to you his open wings,
which launched him from my nest.
I give to you his tender heart,
which beats outside his chest.

I give to you his little light,
now blazing from his soul.
In faith, I give his mother's heart,
the first he ever stole.

He'll always be my little boy,
for all the days l live.
So, this I ask with all I have,
please cherish all I give.

A Million Things

The boy is more than what you see...
A million things, he is to me.

He is:

Bubbles at bath-time, potions of red,
tickles and chuckles and snuggles in bed.
Teeth under pillows, fluffy green dragons,
tricycles, scooters, and shiny red wagons.

Puppies and playdates, scrapes on the knees.
Kisses from Nanny and afternoon teas.
Legends of heroes, wizards, and kings -
he's all that and more; he's a million things.

He is:

Parties and presents, birthday balloons,
lover of ice-cream and licker of spoons.
foamy hot spas and star-gazing nights,
paper plane slipstreams and sky surfing kites.

Spiderman movies, walks through the park,
marsh-mellows roasting on twigs after dark.
Devil of cuteness, angel with wings -
he's all that and more; he's a million things.

He is:

Fantasy author, painter of scenes,
maker of cupcakes and marble machines.
Bow ties and braces, clothed with great flair,
stripy red pants and kaleidoscope hair.

Musical genius, born to achieve,
quirky and sneaky, with tricks up his sleeve.
Master of dungeons, magical rings -
he's all that and more; he's a million things.

He is:

Grandson and nephew, brother, and son,
yet while he's all that, he has barely begun.
That's who he is.
That's what I see.
My boy is a million memories to me.

The End

Thankyou

Thank you to all the people in my life who have walked beside me as I've meandered through motherhood. In particular, I'm grateful for my own Mum, who has invested an enormous amount of time in my boys and in the lives of her other grandchildren. Thanks Mum - your influence on them has had a positive and lasting effect.

To all the mothers I've shared moments and stories with over the years, thank you for your honesty, your ear, the laughs, and the glasses of wine. Motherhood is like Sisterhood – sharing, encouraging, and supporting each other makes a huge difference in challenging times.

Thanks also to those who have followed me on social media. Knowing my writing touches people is what makes it all worthwhile.

If you purchased this book from Amazon, I'd love for you to leave a review with your thoughts.

Catherine Campbell

Printed in Poland
by Amazon Fulfillment
Poland Sp. z o.o., Wrocław